BEDTI  STORIES FOR KIDS

(NEW SERIES)

Fairy Tales, Adventure to Relaxing Night with beautiful Dreams

ROBERT K. CLARK

TABLE OF CONTENTS

Bedtime Stories for Kids
King Midas and the Golden Touch

One day Silenus, the most established of the satyrs who was currently exceptionally powerless, got lost in the grape plantations of King Midas. Somebody discovered him meandering weakly about, scarcely ready to walk, and carried him to the king. Quite a while in the past, Silenus had gone about as attendant and educator to the little wine god, Bacchus. Since Silenus had developed old, Bacchus, thus, dealt with him. So King Midas sent the one who discovered him to convey the satyr securely to Bacchus.

As a trade-off for this generosity, Bacchus vowed to give whatever King Midas may inquire. Ruler Midas knew all around ok what he generally wanted. Back then, kings had depositories in their castles, that is, protected where they could store away important things. The depository of King Midas contained a huge assortment of rich gems, bowls of silver and gold, chests of gold coins, and different things that he thought about valuable.

When Midas was a small kid, he used to watch the subterranean insects running to and fro over the sand close to his dad's royal residence. He couldn't help thinking that the ant colony resembled another castle and that the subterranean insects were buckling down conveying in treasure; for they came racing to the ant colony from all headings, conveying minimal white groups.

Midas decided, then, at that point, that when he grew up, he would buckle down and amass treasures. Since he was a man, and the king, nothing gave him more delight than to add to the assortment in his depository. He was constantly contriving methods of trading or selling different things or making some new assessment for people to pay and transforming everything into gold or silver.

Indeed, he had assembled treasure so persistently, and for such countless years, that he had started to imagine that the dazzling yellow gold in his chests was the most lovely and the most valuable thing on the planet. So when Bacchus offered him anything that he may request, King Midas' originally thought was about his depository, and he asked that whatever he contacted may be transformed into gold. His desire was allowed. Ruler Midas was not really ready to have faith in his favorable luck. He thought himself the most fortunate of men.

At the time his desire was in all actuality, he turned out to be remaining under an oak tree, and the primary thing he did was to lift his hand and contact one of its branches. Quickly the branch turned into the most extravagant gold, with every one of the little oak seeds as awesome and glossy as anyone might think possible. He giggled victoriously at that, and afterward, he contacted a little stone on the ground. This turned into a strong gold chunk. Then, at that point, he picked an apple from a tree, and in his grasp, it turned into a lovely, splendid, gold apple.

Gracious, there was not even a shadow of a doubt: King Midas truly had the Golden Touch! He thought it unrealistic. After this, he contacted the lilies that lined the walk. They abandoned unadulterated white to dazzling yellow, yet bowed their heads lower than at any other time, as though they were embarrassed about the change that the bit of King Midas had given them.

Before transforming additional things into gold, the king took a seat at the little table that his workers had brought out into the court. The corn was new and fresh, and the grapes succulent and sweet. In any case, when he nibbled into a grape from one of the delicious bunches, it turned into a hard wad of gold in his mouth. This was unsavory.

He laid the gold ball on the table and attempted the corn, just to have his mouth loaded up with hard yellow metal. Feeling as though he were gagging, he tasted the water, and at a few his lips even this got fluid gold. His girl strolled towards him, then, at that point began running, with arms out to give him an embrace. In any case, similarly, as her hand contacted him, she, as well, had become a brilliant sculpture.

Out of nowhere the entirety of his brilliant fortunes started to look appalling to him, and his heart developed as weighty as though that, as well, were going to gold. That late evening King Midas set down under a flawless brilliant cover, with his head upon a cushion of strong gold, yet he was unable to rest. Rest would not come to him. As he lay there, he started to expect that his sovereign and all his caring companions may likewise be changed to hard, brilliant sculptures. This would be more loathsome than everything else that had come about because of his stupid desire. Helpless Midas saw since wealth was not the best, however. He was restored perpetually of his affection for gold.

The moment it was sunshine, he raced to Bacchus and asked the god to reclaim his lethal blessing. "Ok," said Bacchus, grinning, "so you have sufficiently gold, finally. Great. If you are certain that you don't wish to transform much else into that metal, proceed to wash in the spring where the stream Pactolus rises. The unadulterated water of that spring will wash away the Golden Touch." King Midas readily complied and became as liberated from the Golden Touch as to when he was a kid watching the subterranean insects. However, the unusual sorcery was moved to the waters of the spring, and right up 'til the present time the stream Pactolus has brilliant sands.

The Ant and the Grasshopper

One warm summer's day a Grasshopper sat on a piece of sod appreciating the daylight. 'What a fine day,' he said. 'The sun's sparkling and I have however much grass that I can eat.' The Grasshopper went through the entire daytime stuffing his face until he was unable to eat something else. 'Right,' he said. 'Presently I'll make some music.'

He scoured his back legs against his wings and made a boisterous humming sound. 'Exquisite,' said the Grasshopper. 'Nothing better than the sound of a cheerful Grasshopper.'

'Give it a rest,' said a passing Ant. 'What?' said the Grasshopper. 'I'm attempting to work here,' said the Ant. 'You're giving me a migraine.' 'You don't care for my music?' said the Grasshopper.

'Not my sort of thing,' said the Ant. 'At any rate ain't got time to remain around discussing music. Got stuff to do.' 'Stuff?' said the Grasshopper. 'What stuff have you had the opportunity to do on a flawless bright morning like this?' 'Gotta get this food moved,' said the Ant. The Grasshopper saw that the Ant was hauling along a colossal ear of corn. 'That appears as though difficult work, mate,' said the Grasshopper.

'Enlighten me concerning it,' said the Ant. 'How you doing it?' said the Grasshopper. 'Taking it to our home,' said the Ant. 'What're you doing that for?' 'Nourishment for the colder time of year,' said the Ant. 'Gotta prepare for the colder time of year.' 'Why?' said the Grasshopper. 'Winter will not come for a long time. It Will is not wintered till...the winter. It's mid-year now. Why stress over the colder time of year?'

'We generally stress over the colder time of year.' said the Ant. 'We burn the entire summer getting together nourishment for the colder time of year. It's what we insects do.' 'It's not what

Grasshoppers do,' said the Grasshopper. 'We Grasshoppers realize how to appreciate the mid-year. Eat...sleep...make some cool music...it's a fine life. We Grasshoppers realize how to live, see.'

'Right,' said the Ant. 'I'll let you have at it.' 'Don't go, Ant, mate,' said the Grasshopper. 'Stick around. Spend the day with me.' 'Sorry.' said the Ant. 'As I said, I got stuff to do.' The Ant hauled his ear of corn and battled off across the field.

'Please yourself,' called the Grasshopper. 'I'm not pestered. I got stuff to do as well. Got this grass to eat. Got the sun to appreciate. Not going to squander an exquisite day like this conversing with insects! Have you at any point seen a more senseless animal than a subterranean insect?' yelled the Grasshopper.

It was winter. The Grasshopper was cold. Too cold to even consider jumping. Too cold to even think about making his music. What's more, he was ravenous. He'd gone the entire day searching for something to eat. Unexpectedly he saw the Ant. 'Hi Ant,' he shuddered. 'Recollect me?' 'That's right,' said the Ant. 'Cold, isn't it?' said the Grasshopper. 'Overall quite warm in our home,' said the Ant. 'Less to eat now is there,' said the Grasshopper.

'We have a bounty,' said the Ant. 'Our storerooms are brimming with seeds and corn. Got heaps of food. Enough to see us securely through to spring.' 'Heaps of food, eh?' said the Grasshopper. 'Look...mate...I don't assume I could...? I don't assume you'd have the option to give me...?' 'You said you'd never seen a more senseless animal than an Ant,' said the Ant.

'I didn't imply that,' said the Grasshopper. 'That was only a joke. Goodness, please. Only a few ears of corn. You can save it. I have nothing.' 'Sorry...mate,' said the Ant. 'Assuming you set aside when you have a bounty, there'll never be a day when you don't have anything.' The Ant rushed down into his warm home realizing that he'd never under any circumstance see that Grasshopper again.

The Bubble Mystery

Honk Toot was extremely glad. She was going to the lake interestingly. Shower time. From the outset, Toot-Toot was frightened of the water. However, when she saw the wide range of various goats sprinkling around, she bounced in. Everybody chuckled. Everybody sprinkled. Everybody played a lot. Honk Toot before long discovered air pockets all around her. They were going blop! She was somewhat apprehensive.

However, she before long got over it. Honk Toot started to hop, dance, and spin through the air pockets. After that pleasant day, Toot-Toot started to ponder, "How are bubbles made?" She asked her Baba. Baba said he didn't have a clue. Honk Toot asked her Ma. Mama said she didn't have a clue, however.

So Toot-Toot chose to tackle the air pocket secret without help from anyone else. She fluttered her tail in the water... She blew into the water energetically... However, she didn't make an air pocket. At some point, Toot-Toot's belly was harming. She thought about what to do. She chose to wash in the lake's cool water.

There was a profound thundering in her belly. Out of nowhere, gas got away from Toot-Toot! Pssshhhhhtttt! As the gas shot through the water rises flew to the water's surface. Blop. At long last, Toot-Toot had addressed the air pocket secret. Presently, at whatever point it's shower day, Toot-Toot makes the most wonderful air pockets of all. After her first shower day, Toot-Toot's sister asked her how air pockets were made. Furthermore, what did Toot-Toot say? Why she revealed to her sister she didn't have a clue.

The Wind And The Sun

Once there was a fight between the sun and the breeze. Each bragged its force. Before long they saw an explorer going out and about. They chose to test their solidarity with him. It concurred that whosoever would make the explorer remove his jacket would be pronounced as the victor and more grounded of the two.

The breeze attempted her strength first. As the breeze blew, the explorer caught his jacket to his body since he was feeling cold. Presently it was the turn of the sun. The sun sparkled splendidly. In this searing warmth of the sun, the voyager started to feel anxious. He was feeling extremely hot. In this way, he removed his jacket, drank some water, and sat under an obscure tree for rest. Subsequently, the breeze fizzled in making the explorer remove his jacket however the sun succeeded.

The Mice That Ate Iron

Quite a long time ago, there was a rich dealer called Naduk. However, times were terrible and his business was languishing. He chose to leave the city and discover his fortune in another spot. He auctions off the entirety of his assets and took care of his obligations. All that he had left was a substantial iron bar. Naduk went to bid farewell to his companion Lakshman and mentioned him to save the shaft for him till he returned. Lakshman vowed to care for it for him.

For a long time, Naduk went all over, building his fortune. Karma was with him, for he became rich indeed. He got back and purchased another house and began his business once more. He went to visit his companion Lakshman who welcomed him heartily. Inevitably, Naduk requested that he return his bar. Lakshman realized that the bar would bring him great cash so he was unwilling to bring it back. So he disclosed to Naduk that he had kept his bar in the store-room and the mice ate it.

Naduk didn't appear to mind. He requested that Lakshman send his child home with him so he could give up a blessing that he had purchased for him. So Lakshman sent his child Ramu with Naduk. Naduk secured up Ramu a basement in his home. By dusk, Lakshamn was stressed and came to ask over the whereabouts of his child. Naduk answered that while heading to his home, a falcon dove down and carted the kid away. Lakshman blamed Naduk for lying. He demanded that a bird of prey couldn't cart away a fifteen-year-old kid.

A major battle followed and the matter was prosecuted. When the judge heard Lakshman's side of the story, he requested Naduk to return the kid to his dad. However, Naduk demanded that a falcon stole away the kid. The officer asked him how it was conceivable. He replied, that if a colossal iron bar can be eaten by mice, a kid could be taken away by a bird of prey. Naduk related the entire story. Everybody in the court burst out giggling. The justice then, at that point requested Lakshman to return the iron shaft to Naduk and that Naduk return Lakshman's child to him.

The Dog And The Elephant

Quite a long time ago in the imperial castle there carried on a regal ruler. The elephant all around took care of and very much dealt with as he was the most cherished creations of the king. There was additionally a helpless canine who was remaining close to the elephant's shed. He was constantly captivated by the smell of the imperial food that was served to the elephant. The helpless canine was not getting any nutritious food and subsequently, it was pale and thin.

One day when the illustrious elephant was resting the canine couldn't avoid the smell of the imperial food and entered the elephant's shed. Helpless canine ate the sweet rice which was left over after the elephant had got done with eating. Sweet rice was one of the most loved dishes of the canine.

For a couple of days, the canine did likewise of eating the extra food of an elephant. The canine also got sound. As he turned out to be large and solid the elephant had the option to see him. Before long both the canine and the elephant turned out to be old buddies. Elephant used to impart all the food to the canine and used to play with him. The canine began to remain in the shed of the elephant. Indeed, even the guardian of the elephant wouldn't fret the canine remaining with the elephant.

One day a rancher who was passing the shed saw the canine and inquired as to whether he could offer the canine to him. The rancher offered a decent cost to the canine. Even though the guardian didn't possess the canine still he offered the canine at an excellent cost.

The elephant turned out to be pitiful after the canine left the shed. He didn't eat any food and turned out to be extremely feeble. He missed his solitary companion the canine a lot and henceforth quit playing, washing, and in any event, eating. The information on the elephants' disintegrating wellbeing arrived at the illustrious castle and the ruler. The king had an astute clergyman in his royal residence. The pastor did an intensive examination of the elephant and said to the overseer that genuinely the elephant had no issues. He further said that likely the elephant is sadness blasted. He inquired as to whether the overseer knows any of his dear companions whom he is absent?

The overseer then, at that point opened up and said that a canine was remaining in a similar shed and both elephant and canine had become dear companions. The guardian further told the pastor that he offered the canines to a rancher and doesn't have a clue where he took him. The clergyman returned to the king and portrayed the entire story. The king was extremely vexed and asked the pastor " how might we get back the canine and fulfill the elephant?" The priest said to make a declaration saying that whoever has the imperial canine will be compensated liberally.

On hearing the declaration the rancher got back the canine quickly to the illustrious castle. The canine ran back to the elephant's shed. The elephant on seeing his companion turned out to be extremely cheerful and both began to play together. The king was glad to see the elephant sound. The pastor was remunerated for his judgment and from that point, both elephant and canine lived joyfully together.

A Merchant and His Donkey

One wonderful spring morning, a shipper stacked his jackass with sacks of salt to go to the market, to sell the salt. The dealer and his jackass were strolling along together. They had not strolled far when they arrived at a stream coming. Tragically, the jackass slipped and fell into the waterway. As it mixed up the bank of the stream, it saw that the packs of salt stacked on his back had gotten lighter. There was nothing the vendor could do aside from getting back, where he stacked his jackass with more packs of salt. As they arrived at the elusive riverbank once more, the jackass fell into the stream, this time purposely.

Consequently, the salt was squandered once more. At this point, the trader knew the jackass' stunt. He needed to show the creature something new. As he got back the second time with the jackass, the vendor stacked sacks of wipes on its back. The couple set out on their outing to the market a third time. On arriving at the stream, the jackass cunningly fell into the water once more. However, presently, rather than the heap getting lighter, it got heavier.

The Lonely Snowmen

Mid one cold December morning, following a snowstorm the night before, a mother, father, and their two kids, a child, and girl, went outside into the back nursery to play in the recently settled snow. Mother was as yet in her mid-20's, she had wavy earthy colored hair with light green eyes and light composition, father was two years more established than mother, a serious stocky man, who might consistently have his hair searched over to one side, his eyes were a bizarre dull blue.

Their child was just seven, he would get up in the first part of the day and attempt to style his light earthy colored hair like his dads yet like his mom he had light green eyes and her composition, he was conceived two minutes before his sister who's hair was just somewhat wavy. Their girl had light blue eyes which they accepted would develop more obscure like her dad's yet she was more modest than her sibling and consistently preferred to wear a French beret.

A couple of hours passed as they played before mother called "kids might you want to make a snowman", with extraordinary delight and energy the kids cheerfully concurred. Father surged inside snatching his old cap, an extra scarf that had been sewn for him by his sister, a carrot several catches. When he returned out the kids were attempting to fold the snow into a huge ball for the snowman's base, father snickering chose to assist and put the stuff down before rapidly surging over to loan his hand.

Mother was on the telephone yet before long set it aside as the kids and father chose to drop a heap of snow over her, they went around the snowman's base, mother laughing like a young lady once more, father laughing with his profound voice, the kids again began to attempt roll the following ball for the snowman's top half. Mother and father seeing this started to help the little kids who were resolved to make the snowman, at long last they were finished with the base for their snowman, "would we be able to put on the cap and scarf father, please" argued the kids,

"Obviously" laughed father as he pulled mother nearer to accept her in an energetic kiss, as everything for him felt great, he had his lovely spouse, he's caring kids and they all functioned admirably together. It was easy wasn't difficult to see mom's happiness as she grinned consistently at her lovely children working away with cheer. The kids were just about ready to get the scarf on however were incapable to arrive at the head to put the cap on the snowman, father seeing this chuckled a little before getting the kid so he could arrive at the snowman's head.

Mother got the catches and carrot, putting them on the snowman to make his eyes and nose, the kids dashed off before getting back with three sticks, two a similar size and one significantly more limited, they put the two sticks on the sides of the snowman to make arms and father bowed the more modest one to make the snowman's grin.

They all remained back, father accepting mother and the two kids remained in front, all appreciating their work of adoration, before heading back inside to eat. What they hadn't understood is that their unadulterated love and energy had come off on the snowman rejuvenating him, he stood there briefly his heart loaded up with such a lot of satisfaction and empathy, he felt like a part of the family and all he knew was love, however that is all he believed he required.

Ordinarily, for seven days after that the children and in some cases mother and father would come to join the party, continually welcoming the snowman, the kids would go around him and converse with him some of the time, which mother and father discovered entertaining, however, the snowman was euphoric that they liked him so much and that they cherished him, he was genuinely disdain.

Then, at that point, an incredible snowstorm came and the kids weren't permitted outside to play, yet the snowman remained in a similar spot pausing, realizing that they would ultimately return to play with him. A day passed by, then, at that point another, then, at that point seven days, then, at that point fourteen days, still nobody came outside to visit the snowman, however, he was certain they would ultimately.

Very nearly a month passed before the kids got back to play, the snowman's heart was inspired to see the kids' glad appearances traveled his direction, however they passed directly past him without a solitary look toward him, he hearts sunk, 'for what reason aren't they coming to play by me?' he addressed, obviously his mouth being only a stick which had lost its curve he was unable to talk.

He watched and hung tight for them to come and play by him or welcome him yet they didn't Every day after that when they would come to join the party his heart would ascend as they drew near however sink again as they went on with their pleasant leaving him to remain in his side of the nursery.

The climate before long started to change the colder time of year was leaving and spring was starting to enter the nursery, however, the snowman wouldn't soften away just his head had sunk a bit, he put stock in his true inner being that they would recollect him, his psyche consistently returned to that day they made him, when they were so pleased with him and how he ended up and the happy looks on their appearances when they used to view him.

Then, at that point one day while he remained there watching the house, the snow surrounding him had essentially transformed into a wet ooze, however, he actually stood there solid, the kids came outside with mother and father, from the outset they circumvented their typical propensities for going around playing with one another while he remained there expecting their affection once more. The young lady was running from her sibling before winding up before the snowman, "Mother" she called, "For what reason is the snowman still there?",

I"don't have a clue about, who cares nectar, he'll dissolve in the long run" she answered tenderly to her girl, yet to the snowman, this was disastrous like somebody had stuck a wine tool into his heart and started bending, "Dear, remember to get the cap and scarf from him before we go in" mother proceeded before returning to her good times.

That evening the snowman stood their hatless and without his scarf, he needed to cry yet his catches had no tear conduits, so he remained there desolate cold and grief-stricken, his stick had no lips or tongue so the solitary way he could articulate his thoughts was in his musings. The following morning the kids came outside to play, not in any event, seeing that where the snowman once stood was a puddle of water, his adoration for them had been his demise, that was the last anybody saw of the once cherished snowman, presently the desolate snowman.

The Musical Donkey

When a washerman had a jackass. During the day, the jackass needed to convey weighty heaps of garments, yet around evening time it was allowed to meander about. However it was old and frail, it adored wandering in the fields. One evening, the jackass met a jackal. They became companions and went looking for food. They discovered a field loaded with ready cucumbers. They ate however many cucumbers as they could. The following evening, they again devoured the cucumbers in the field.

From that point onward, the two companions would go to a nursery consistently. Before long the jackass developed fat. One night it said to be jackal "Look, my dear, the full moon is sparkling in the sky. A delicate breeze is blowing. It is wonderful. I want to bawl." The jackal was savvy. He exhorted the jackass not to whinny as it would welcome difficulty. However, the jackass didn't pay attention to his recommendation and began whinnying. The jackal was adequately shrewd to getaway.

On hearing the bawling of the jackass, the ranchers hurried to the spot, outfitted with sticks. They gave the jackass an intensive beating and left it half-dead. After some time, the jackal returned. He praised the jackass for the award that it had got for singing to the moon.

The City Rat and a Village Rat

Once two rodents were old buddies. One of them lived in a city and the other lived in a town. The two of them traded information on their prosperity through other city rodents and the town retreats who went between the two spots. When the city rodent wished to meet his town companion. He sent the message through certain rodents of the town. The town companion was extremely amped up for his companions' visit. He made arrangements to invite him.

To accept his companion, he went to the line of the town wearing a customary dress like dhoti, kurta, and cap, with a wreath in his grasp. Notwithstanding, his city companion was wearing a suit, boots, and a necktie. They embraced one another and traded welcoming. The town rodent invited him and said, "We have new and unpolluted air here. The air in the city is unclean."

They tattled a great deal and traded their perspectives on various themes. Then, at that point, they plunked down to eat.

The town rodent served him leafy foods wheat grains. In the wake of having food, they took a walk around the town. The fields looked green and the regular excellence of the wilderness had its fascination. The town rodent said, "Does the city have such lovely scenes?" The city rodent said only welcomed the town rodent to go to the city essentially once to see the agreeable existence of the city.

The town rodent said he would surely go to the city one day. The city rodent said, "Why not go with me now?" The town rodent answered, "Okay, I will think about your proposition." When the night fell, they returned and rested on the delicate grass. The following day, for breakfast, the town rodent served his companion new foods grown from the ground. The city rodent was disturbed and said to the town rodent, "Let us go to the city at this moment. Allow me an opportunity to serve you."

The town rodent acknowledged the proposition and prepared for the excursion to the city. The city rodent lived in a major house. Around evening time the town rodent was astonished to see, the eating table loaded with various sorts of dishes. The town rodent has not seen such an assortment of food previously. The city rodent asked the town rodent to appreciate the dinner. Then, at that point, he began eating. The town rodent had a preference for the paneer and completed the piece rapidly. As of now, they heard the voice of a cat.

The city rodent said, "Rapidly conceal yourself underneath the almirah, in any case, the cat will eat us." Both hurried to the almirah and shrouded themselves under it. After some time, when the cat disappeared, both came out. The town rodent was all the while shuddering. The city rodent again began eating the dishes and prompted his companion as well, "Don't be apprehensive. It is a piece of the city life." The town rodent assembled fortitude and went to the eating table once more. This time he immediately completed his preferred cake.

At this point, a kid came there with a canine. The town rodent fearing the canine asked his companion, "Who is this person?" The city rodent said, "He is Jimmi, the child of the expert of this house and the canine is his pet. Be fast and conceal yourself there." After their takeoff, both the rodents came out. The town rodent was extremely apprehensive. He said, "Companion, I figure I should return now. I'm appreciative to you for the delectable dishes, yet there are too numerous risks. Much appreciated once more." And he began for the town. On coming to, he hurled a murmur of help and said, "Gracious! Life is valuable or more all intelligence."

The Blue Jackal

Quite a long time ago there was a jackal who has been more daring and habitually wandered into the town searching for food. The Village was loaded up with canines and the jackal was terrified of them. They made certain to kill him or mischief him seriously if they at any point figured out how to catch him. In any case, the fascination of food demonstrated excessively solid for him and the jackal made a trip to the city over and over.

One day similarly as he planned to go into a major house he heard the sound of loud woofing. To his shock, he discovered a pack of canines running towards the house. They looked rough and the jackal was before long shaking in alarm. He ran higgledy-piggledy and tumbled just inside a tub of blue color. The canines skipped him and ran another way. When the jackal moved out of the tub he was colored blue from head to toe.

He showed up truly surprising and unique about some other creature. The jackal was satisfied. "Nobody will actually want to remember me now" he advised himself, "I could without much of a stretch dolt anybody in the wilderness. " When he entered the woodland indeed everyone was stunned to see a particularly peculiar creature. There had never seen any creature of that tone previously.

"Who right? " the more modest creatures asked him. "Where have you come from?" asked the strong lion with a glare. "Did anybody send you? " scrutinized the furious tiger giving him an exciting look. "God has sent me to take care of you," said the blue jackal in a colossal voice, "I'll be your king from this point forward. " "However I have consistently been the ruler of the backwoods" fought the powerful lion.

"All that should change now as I am simply the king," said the blue jackal living it up, "every one of you should serve me and do precisely as I advise you." "Imagine a scenario where we don't?" asked the tiger. "Then, at that point, God will crush the entire woodland and every one of you with it," said the blue jackal. Different creatures didn't set out to say much else. "What might you like us to do?" they asked the blue jackal. "Bring me heaps of food, first and foremost," said the blue jackal instantly. Every one of the creatures surged off in different ways. In a brief time frame, they were back with bunches of food. They took care to bring anything they could discover and offered the best of everything to the blue jackal.

The jackal was enchanted and had his fill. There was considerably more food than he could eat. "Presently everyone can gobble up the remainder of the food," he said, "Yet mind you, you need to bring me new food day by day. " The creatures guaranteed to serve him reliably. He assigned unique duties to every one of the creatures yet exiled the bunch of jackals from the timberland since he was hesitant they could recognize him sometime in the future.

The blue jackal had an amazing second subsequently. He didn't have to leave the timberland or hazard confronting the canines and presently got the absolute best of everything without taking any kind of action. He giggled without help from anyone else each time he recalled precisely how sagaciously he had tricked the part – including the tiger, the strong elephant, and the lion who respected themselves ridiculously fabulous. However, one day something unpredicted occurred. The restricted bunch of jackals was strolling around right external the woodland and cried aggregately noisily. The blue jackal neglected himself and went along with them the crying similarly as he used to do previously.

Different creatures were available when it occurred and took a gander at him suspiciously. Here was their powerful blue king wailing like a jackal! So he was a jackal however and not an uncommon creature sent from heaven! He had just shaded himself by one way or another and had been tricking every one of them nowadays! Tricking the lion king, the intense tiger, and the incredible elephant. They were not going to be deceived any longer. They fell upon the blue jackal and obliterated him before he could explain or even dissent. Also, that was the finish of the blue jackal's standard as lord.

The Clever Rooster

There was an astute fox in timberland. Once, he was meandering in the woods too? discover his food. Abruptly, he spotted fine, fat chicken situated on the part of a high tree, taking a gander at the thick woods around him. The fox understood that he was unable to ascend the tree to kill the chicken, thus he contemplated, "How might I get this chicken for my feast? If l basically demand him to descend, he will generally doubt my thought processes. "

The fox thought about a stunt. He cleverly asked the chicken, "Dear pal, for what reason would you say you are sitting so high on the tree? Is it accurate to say that you fear someone? Do you not actually know what the king of the woods has chosen in a gathering of creatures today? " The chicken said guiltlessly, "No, I have no idea of that. Please explain to me the ruler's choice. " The fox proceeded, "The judgment is that from now onwards, pets or creatures and birds won't kill each other for dinners. Greater? fish won't eat more modest fish. "

The chicken detected that something was truly off-base. This couldn't be valid. He asked, "Does that mean the lions, tigers, and panthers will start benefiting from grass from today? " The fox had positively no response for this. However, he would not like to surrender so without any problem.

He said, "I can see you're not guaranteed. Descend, let us go to the King and request the explanation of this point. He will answer our inquiries. However, he has chosen this for the well-being of everyone. " The chicken was sufficiently keen to perceive the fox's stunt. He said, "You are right, we should visit the King concerning explanation. For what reason do we not take together some more mates with us? It will be more valuable if at any time more creatures will come to think about this choice. "

Imagining that he had prevailed in his technique, the fox said, "Indeed, indeed, why not? We can take some different creatures along. Above all, you descend, then, at that point, we can search for them. " The fox was anticipating that the rooster should come down. He was invigorated. Out of nowhere, the chicken said, "We are fortunate, we don't need to look for different companions. I can see a couple of your companions are only showing up at this side. They are going to arrive at this spot. We can take them along".

The fox said, "Goodness, that is acceptable! Yet, who are these animals? " The chicken answered, "I can see an enormous number of dogs moving toward. I trust they are incredible companions with you? " "Dogs! " the fox hollered in alarm. He began running for a valuable life. The chicken addressed, "For what reason would you say you are running at this point? You have quite recently educated me that each of the creatures and birds has become old buddies with each other. " The fox replied, "However likely the dogs may conceivably not have caught wind of this judgment. " He fled into the thick timberland. The chicken snickered on the fox's moronic methodology. Every one of the birds unwinding on the tree cheered the chicken's humor.

A Wolf and Seven Lambs

Some time ago, a goat was living close to the timberland. She had seven children and cherished them a great deal. At some point, the goat needed to bring nourishment for her children. She needed to go to the timberland. He cautioned her children, "Never open the entryway for anybody. The eyes of the wolf are on us." She bid farewell to her children and got out.

The wolf was watching the hovel of the goat. His #1 food was sheep tissue. When he saw the goat leaving, he promptly went to the hovel and thumped on the entryway, "Hello there, Kids. It is Mom. If it's not too much trouble, open the entryway. I purchased nourishment for you." The children were sharp, and they comprehended that I wasn't their mom. They said, "You are not the mother. You can't trick us! Disappear!"

The wolf attempted to counterfeit the voice of the goat. After rehearsing for some time, he went to the hovel and thumped on the entryway once more, "Hi kids! Open the entryway. Mother is here!". The children were shrewd in this way, they looked outside through the wizardry glass of the entryway. They perceived the feet of the wolf and said, "No chance! We won't open the entryway.

Your feet are unique to mothers. Her feet are white." The wolf heard this and went to the merchant's shop. He needed him to shade his feet to white with flour. The food merchant failed to really see why the wolf needed this, yet he did what the wolf said as he feared. Accordingly, the feet of the wolf got white. He quickly went to the cabin of goat and thumped on the entryway, "Hi kids! It is the mother. Open the entryway!"

The children again peeped through the wizardry glass and saw the white feet. They opened the entryway. The wolf got in. When they see the wolf, they raced to conceal someplace. Some covered up under the bed, some in the background. The wolf got them and ate them up. Nonetheless, one of the children stowed away within the large clock. The wolf couldn't discover him. The mother goat was going to arrive at the hovel.

She was imagining that the children would be glad to see the food sources. She came to after some time. In any case, she was stunned when she saw the entryway open. She got in and couldn't perceive any of her children. She began to cry and said "What befell you? My helpless children! I said you not to open the entryway. The wolf gobbled up you. I lost all of you."

At that point, the child who stowed away within the clock spoke, "Mother! It is me, your most youthful child. I'm on the clock. Take me out." The goat took out her child and kissed him over and over. The child determined what befell different children. Then, at that point, they heard a wheezing. The mother said, "The wolf should be still here. Discover me long scissors and brought it." They discovered the wolf dozing in the nursery. The goat drew near to the wolf quietly and cut open his tummy with the scissors. She discovered her children alive and afterward took them out personally. In the wake of kissing and embracing them, she needed them to discover stones.

The children brought the stones and put them inside the gut of the wolf. Then, at that point, the goat sewed the midsection and got back to the hovel. After some time, woke up and needed to drink water. He went to the well to drink water. Since his paunch was loaded with stones, he lost his equilibrium and fell into the well. He suffocated in the water. The goat and the children were watching the wolf through the window of the cabin. They came out and began moving because they disposed of the wolf and didn't should fear it any longer.

The King And The Drum

Sometime in the distant past there carried on a ruler in focal India. He was attractive yet vain. He took a gander at himself continually, in mirrors, in pools of water, even in others' eyes when they addressed him. "I'm the most handsome King on Earth." He said to his subjects. He tried to ignore administering his realm than he did to have his hair styled and his body rubbed. Therefore, his kin became less fortunate and unhappier. However, the king couldn't have cared less. "Why!" he flaunted one day in court, "I'm presumably more attractive than every one of the divine beings." Unfortunately for the ruler, an especially disagreeable god turned out to be flying by, and was exasperated at what he heard.

"Something should be done about this ruler." He looked to him for a suitable discipline. Then, at that point, his eyes fell upon a bull. "Horns!" The god applauded his hand with malevolent merriment. "I'll perceive how his comeliness likes himself with horns." When the king got up the following morning, he followed his ordinary daily schedule. In the first place, he drew his mirror free from his cushion and looked into it. Abruptly the gatekeepers outside the king's chamber heard a boisterous screech. They came hurrying in to discover the ruler sitting upstanding in bed with a huge cushion on his head.

"Out…. Out… " he waved a shuddering finger at them. As they stepped back, he yelled after them, "Send for the imperial hairdresser right away." The regal stylist was a nervy chatty little man. He came in energetically. "You're up early today, Your Majesty, yet why the pi… " The king broke in, "Stop your patter and approach my body." As the astonished hairstylist moved close, the ruler said in his most ordering voice, "Hairdresser, I'm going to show you something. However, if you talk about it to a solitary living soul, I will have you flagellated and hanged." The ruler gradually eliminated the pad from his head.

"Goodness!" The hairdresser applauded to his mouth with sickening apprehension. "However, don't simply remain there", said the ruler restlessly. "Effectively cover them up." The hairdresser pulled the ruler's hair thusly and that and figured out how to cover the horns somewhat. The king put his nightcap on to conceal the rest. "Presently proceed to tell the court I am unwell. I won't see anybody."

He sat up and scowled at the hairstylist, "And recall my admonition." The hairdresser escaped. When the entryway of the bedchamber shut behind him, he began chuckling. People of royal residence halted and asked him the justification his jollity. However, the stylist just shook his head weakly and ran chuckling through the lobbies.

"I will bite the dust if I don't tell somebody," he moaned. "My stomach is expanding with the mystery." He saw a tamarind tree remaining in the imperial patio. He went ready and murmured the key to its trunk. That evening there was a savage tempest and the Tamarind tree was blown down. The ruler was educated through the entryway, for he would not see anybody, and he instructed the tree to be given to the regal performer. "Allow him to make a drum from the storage compartment of the tamarind and play it outside my entryway."

Before long the drum made of tamarind wood was prepared. The squires collected external the king's entryway and the performer started to play. Yet, rather than the thumthum-thum that everybody expected, the Tamarind drum articulated,

"The Raja has horns on his head. The Raja has horns on his head." The court burst out giggling and the king cried with rage. "I will not remain in the royal residence a second more", he yelled, "I'll go to the backwoods and live without help from anyone else."

He detached the nightcap from his head and ran out of the royal residence, holding onto the Tamarind drum in transit out. The ruler lived for quite a while in the timberland. He figured out how to really focus on animals less than himself. He developed further and shrewd and magnanimous. His solitary buddy was the Tamarind drum and the drum, when he beat it, offered him all the guidance and experience of the old tree. The king figured out how to play the drum so flawlessly that even the spirits of the trees were enchanted and they went to meet the god who had given him the horns.

"Pardon him", they argued. "He has changed. Eliminate his horns and give him back his realm." The god waved his hand and the horns vanished. During the day, the ruler went down to the woods pool to drink water. While measuring his hands he saw his appearance, and his lean, sun-tanned face glanced back at him, with no horns! Furthermore, as he sat up in shock, a few pony riders burst into the clearing and he saw his squires. They bowed before him. "Your Majesty, pardon us and return. The realm needs you." The king returned to his realm. He kept his Tamarind drum alongside him generally and he governed carefully. Also, indeed, the hairstylist kept his head, yet lost his employment.

A Wise Parrot

Some time ago, there was an excellent parrot who lived in a wilderness with his sibling. The parrot was lovely and lived joyfully with his sibling. A tracker was going through a wilderness one day and saw the pair of delightful parrots on a tree. He said, "The parrots are so wonderful. I should give them as a present to the ruler." He chose to get the delightful parrots and made a snare. The parrots were trapped in the snare on the double and the tracker was extremely cheerful. The tracker took the parrots and introduced them to the ruler as a blessing. The king was glad to see the parrots.

He acknowledged the blessing from the tracker and put the parrots in a brilliant confine. The workers were requested to deal with the parrots. The workers used to deal with the parrots and would offer them flavorful food. The parrots were dealt with well and the workers took outrageous consideration of them. The youthful ruler would come to play with the parrots. The sovereign treated them with the most extreme love. He wanted to play with them.

The parrots were glad to get such a lot of adoration and love from the ruler. They were given everything without really busy. One of the parrots said, "We are fortunate to have been brought here." The other parrot answered, "Indeed, we are carrying on with a serene and agreeable life in the royal residence, and with that, we are being adored as well." They both were glad about their lives.

They were the primary fascination of the castle and everybody adored them. All was great until one day the tracker who had gotten them the royal residence got back with another present for the ruler. This time, the tracker carried a dark monkey with him. The king was glad to get the present. He joyfully acknowledged the blessing from the tracker.

Slowly, the monkey turned into the primary fascination in the royal residence. He was adored by everybody and the workers dealt with the monkey and took care of him tasty food. The workers on occasion neglected to take care of the parrots. The youthful sovereign began playing with the monkey. He even focused on the monkey and poor people's parrots were ignored.

The parrots felt terrible. The more youthful parrot said, "The monkey has demolished our lives. No one pays special mind to us any longer." The more seasoned sibling answered, "Don't stress younger sibling. Nothing is lasting in this world. All that will change soon." The monkey was wicked and dynamic. At some point, he made a ton of issues in the castle for everybody. Workers were tired of the monkey and the youthful ruler feared the wicked dark monkey.

At some point, the king requested to toss the monkey out in the wilderness. The monkey was tossed in the wilderness. Presently, again the parrots turned into the focal point of fascination of the castle. Everybody began focusing on the parrots. The parrots were exceptionally glad as their pleasant days were back. The more youthful sibling acknowledged what his senior sibling advised him. "Time never remains something very similar," the more youthful sibling said.

The senior sibling answered, "See, I disclosed to you nothing is lasting. You ought to never get discouraged on terrible occasions." The more youthful sibling then, at that point chose to never become upset on awful occasions or troublesome conditions.

A Talkative Barber

Some time ago there was a tailor in a city. He was jaunty and progressive. He used to call people to his home and described their astonishing stories. People paid attention to his accounts with incredible interest. There was a hair salon close to his store. The stylist was loquacious. People knew his propensity for tattling and frequently making the most of his tattles. At some point, a weak outsider came before the tailor's shop. The outsider came before the tailor's shop.

The outsider was worn out and needed to take a rest. The tailor had sympathy for him and requested that he rest for some time in his shop. The man was appreciative. Out of nowhere, he saw the hairstylist and turned out to be dismal. He said to the tailor, "I'm furious with this hairdresser as he has demolished my life. I disdain him and can't remain here any longer."

The tailor asked him, "For what reason are you so irate with him?" The outsider took a long breath and portrayed his story to the tailor: "my dad was a rich money manager of Baghdad.

After his passing, I was the lone beneficiary of all the abundance he had. I was an unhitched male deeply and didn't care for a lady."

At some point, while I was passing along a street, I saw a lovely young lady remaining at the window of a house. I went gaga for her at the main sight. Simultaneously, I speculated him as the dad of the young lady and immediately left the spot, yet couldn't fail to remember the young lady. I needed to wed her. I unveiled my adoration to one of the companions of my mom. She said, "I know the young lady. She is too pleased and her dad is the adjudicator of the District Court. You may always be unable to win her heart. However, relax. I will help you and converse with her."

She went to the young lady and communicated my longing to her. However, the young lady would not like to meet me. However, after much influence, she called me on Friday after her dad had gone to the mosque for supplication. I was glad and anxious to meet her. I started promptly in the first part of the day on Friday. I called this stylist to shave my facial hair. I requested that he finish his work rapidly, yet the hairstylist was talking consistently. I chided him and said, "Pick up the pace; I need to go to meet somebody."

Yet, the stylist didn't mind by any means. Leaving the shave in the middle, he went out to see the sun and returned at some point. He said, "Today is not a decent day for you and consequently, don't go out to meet anybody." I yelled at him, "Quit rambling! Finish your work and disappear."

Yet, the stylist proceeded ridiculously and said, "I'm not a standard hairdresser. I thoroughly understand the future. I need to help you." I asked him, "Disappear and never return." But the hairstylist didn't go. He hung tight for quite a while and again said, "My king, I came here just when you called me. I will shave your facial hair and afterward, I will accompany you."

Then, at that point, he began shaving my facial hair. Yet, he continued talking ceaselessly. He asked me, "Disclose to me where you are going." I would not like to come clean with him. Henceforth, I lied that I planned to meet my companions. I had been sick and presently had recuperated. So I needed to treat my companions. It would be a major banquet." Suddenly, he quit shaving and said truly, "Expert, I have likewise welcomed my companions for a blowout today. I failed to remember that I needed to buy some food from them." "Be speedy, I will give you nourishment for your companions. Finish your work quick," I said since I was in a rush.

Without hanging tight for an answer, he began moving, and said, "Go to my home and appreciate the organization of my companions. They will engage you. Visit your companions some other day." I giggled at him. He was excessively loquacious. I advised him, "I would be glad to go to your home. However, today it's anything but conceivable because I need to meet my companions. I will go to your home later." The hairstylist said, "It doesn't make any difference if you can't go to my home. I might want to go with you to your companions.

I will offer food to my companions." I cried, "Be speedy and shave." At last, he shaved my facial hair. I advised him, "My workers will give you nourishment for your companions, you can take my workers with you and go at this point." He disappeared. I prepared and left to meet the young lady. I was glad to meet her. It was not in my insight that the hairdresser had followed me. Before long we understood that her dad had returned sooner than expected. She was astonished. When I peeped from the window, I saw the stylist sitting across the street.

In the meantime, her dad went into the house. He blew up with his work on some matter and began beating him. The worker cried in torment. The boisterous cry, made the stylist feel that I was being beaten, consequently, he yelled for help. People assembled around the young lady's home. The hairstylist asked her dad for what valid reason was he beating his king, for example, me. The dad couldn't get anything and said, "What jabber would you say you are talking? Who is your king? I don't have the foggiest idea about your king."

The hairstylist said, "My king is with your girl. Do you realize they love one another? I thought you have requested that your workers beat my king. At any rate, leave my king." The young lady's dad said, "There is nobody in my home. Come inside and see with your own eyes." The stylist went into the house along with people accumulated and began looking for me all over. I had covered up myself inside a crate, however, the hairstylist saw it. He opened the crate and discovered me there.

He yelled and pulled in the consideration of people. I hopped from the crate and ran out of the house. As I was in a rush, I crashed into a stone and fell on the ground, and broke my leg. From that point forward, I am a disabled person. People began following me and to stop them, I tossed gold and silver coins behind me.

However the others halted to pick the coins, the hairstylist kept on after me. Seeing the hairdresser behind me, I took cover in a hotel and asked the proprietor not to permit the stylist to enter. He halted the stylist on the entryway. From that point forward I disdain the stylist. He has ruined my life.

After this, the outsider moved up and disappeared. From there on, the tailor asked the stylist "Was this man feeling reality?" The hairdresser said, "He was correct. I attempted to help him yet he loathed me. I needed to disclose his romantic tale and out of disgrace, the adjudicator would have permitted him to wed his little girl. However, he didn't get me."

The Pied Piper Of Hamelin

Sometime in the distant past, there was a town called Hamelin. Hamelin was a prosperous town. It was a port town on the River Weser. Barges loaded with corn would descend the River Weser and dump at Hamelin. Storehouses were brimming with corn in Hamelin. Barges brimming with wheat would come up the River Weser and dump at Hamelin. Storehouses were brimming with wheat in Hamelin.

With the storehouses brimming with corn and wheat came factories for crushing the corn and wheat, pastry kitchens for heating bread and cakes, looks for selling the bread and cakes, and obviously people for eating. People were so prosperous and caught up with stacking and dumping, processing, preparing, and eating that they didn't see all the litter and junk that was gathering on the roads. Also, obviously with the trash came the rodents.

There were rodents wherever in Hamelin - rodents in the corn storehouses, rodents in the wheat storehouses, rodents in the bread kitchens, rodents in the shops, rodents in the roads, and rodents in the houses. The rodents reproduced and developed and developed and reared and soon there were such countless rodents that life turned out to be very hopeless for the residents of Hamelin. They couldn't heat a cake, wash up, or rest in their beds without the rodents participate. The rodents even snacked on the ears of children dozing in their beds.

Something must be finished. People of Hamelin advanced toward the Town Square and thumped on the huge metal entryways of the Town Hall and requested to know what the King Mayor was doing about the rodents. The King Mayor showed up on the gallery in his dark robes and gold chains and gave a discourse.

"Productive members of society of Hamelin you may have confidence that what should be done is being finished. Don't you stress over that?" The productive members of the society of Hamelin weren't excessively certain about that however they returned home to their homes to perceive what might be finished. However, nothing was finished. There was the same amount of trash on the roads and similarly as numerous rodents in the plants, the bread kitchens, the shops, and the houses. Truth be told there were more rodents.

The rodents continued developing and rearing and reproducing and developing and eating and eating and eating. They ate anything they could get their teeth on. Nothing or nobody was protected from the rodents. People were furious and walked to the Town Square and beat on the large metal entryways and to know precisely what the King Mayor planned to do. When no King Mayor showed up in the gallery. People began to recite - "No rodents!" "No rodents!" "No rodents!" "No rodents!"

At last, the King Mayor showed up on the overhang in his dark robes and gold chains and reported to some degree anxiously that he had a positive strategy. "Productive members of society of Hamelin you will satisfy to realize that I, the King Mayor, have provided orders that a huge opening in the ground will be burrowed on the edges of Hamelin and into that opening will be cleared the entirety of the trash in the roads and the entirety of the rodents that can be found and killed. Before long Hamelin will be spotless and clear of rodents."

Before long the enormous opening in the ground was brimming with smelling waste and the collections of dead rodents and quickly covered over with soil. Yet, it was insufficient there was an excessive number of rodents in too many concealing spots everywhere in the town and a lot of nourishment for them in the storehouses and bread kitchens and shops and houses and they developed and reproduced and reared and became similarly as quick as in the past. What's more, presently with the rodents came a plague of insects.

Furthermore, with the insects came a weird ailment. A few kids and elderly folks people had as of now kicked the bucket. A plague was on Hamelin. As you can envision people of Hamelin were significantly angrier. They walked again to the town square. Every one of them conveyed with them twelve dead rodents as confirmation of the disappointment of the King Mayors plan. They tossed the rodents in a heap in the square and from a shaft they hung a likeness that looked amazingly like the King Mayor in his dark robes and his gold chains.

They began reciting - "No Rats or no Mayor!" "No Rats or no Mayor!" "No Rats or no Mayor!" When the King Mayor came out on his overhang he was encircled by his Councilors and he reported rather anxiously that the committee had, considering the somewhat urgent circumstance, consented to offer a sublime prize of 1,000 gold guilders to any person who could free the town of the rodents.

The following day an outsider showed up in Hamelin. He was distinctive from every other person. His garments were beautiful and appeared to come from a wide range of spots. He wore a cap covered with quills and shells and bones. From a long scarf hung a silver line.

The outsider followed the trucks up from the port and he saw the storehouses loaded with corn and the storehouses brimming with wheat and the factories and pastry kitchens and shops and houses and people and trash and the rodents. He strolled unobtrusively to the Town Square and thumped on the enormous metal entryways of the Town Hall. He told the Mayor and his councilors that for 1,000 gold guilders he could free Hamelin of the rodents that invaded it. The Mayor excitedly concurred and the Pied Piper ventured outside.

He remained in the Square and glanced unobtrusively around. He took a full breath and blew a note on his silver line that addressed the rodents of faraway places, of woods and backwoods and rocks and mountains. He blew another note that addressed the rodents of foxes and wolves and falcons and birds. He blew the third note and the entirety of the rodents in Hamelin began to run towards the Pied Piper.

They rushed out of entryways, out of windows, out of channels, and out of openings. They hurried down the paths and roads towards the square. Presently the Pied Piper began to play a moving tune and he moved out of the square and the rodents tracked with behind. They moved out of the town and towards the port.

At the waterway side, the Piper halted and he set only one toe in the water and, as he kept playing, the rodents kept moving across the wharves and into the stream. Rodents by their thousands moved out of the town, across the wharves, and sprinkled into the waterway where they were suffocated.

When the last one had vanished underneath the waters of the Weser the Pied Piper halted.

He stood discreetly taking a gander at the water for some time and afterward turned and strolled back to the Town Square. The great people of Hamelin were commending the triumph against the rodents. Finally, they were liberated from the epidemic. The King Mayor and the entirety of his Councilors were up on their overhang slapping each other on the back and making discourses. The Pied Piper sat tight for a calm space and requested his 1,000 gold guilders.

The Mayor called out so everybody could hear, "1,000 gold guilders? How is it possible that you would have perhaps acquired 1,000 guilders? Why. Everybody perceived how, while the rodents were suffocating themselves in the waterway, everything you did was a dance about and play on that senseless little line of yours. Here be happy with forty guilders and think yourself fortunate at that."

To the disgrace of people of Hamelin, they concurred with their Mayor and chuckled at the Pied Piper as he strolled discreetly out of the town. The following day was a strict gala and the entirety of the grown-ups were in the congregation as he strolled once more into the town. He stood unobtrusively for some time in the Town Square and they slowly inhaled and played a note that addressed the offspring of distant spots, clean air, and starting waterways.

He blew another note that addressed the offspring of pointless fooling around and whales and dolphins and brilliantly shaded parrots. He blew the third note and the entirety of the kids began to run and bounce and jump out of the houses towards the Town Square. As they ran and bounced and skipped towards him the Pied Piper began to move out of the square towards the port.

The grown-ups in the congregation heard the entirety of the kids go past and they hurried out of the congregation to perceive what was occurring. They shouted to the kids to pause and to return yet it resembled they could at this point don't hear their folks' voices. The parents were calmed when they saw the Pied Piper get some distance from the stream and hit the dance floor with the kids towards the mountain. Their help went to repulsiveness however when a little entryway showed up in the side of the mountain and first the Pied Piper and afterward the kids began to run and hop and skirt inside.

The parents approached to stop them however it was past the point of no return. The entirety of the kids bar one kid who was jumping along on props and couldn't keep up vanished inside the mountain and the little entryway pummeled shut so firmly that nobody could tell precisely where it had been. People hustled up with digging tools and picks and began angrily delving openings in the mountainside yet it was all without much of any result. The little kid on props attempted to advise them of the hints of faraway places, clean air, and starting waterways and silly buffoonery and whales and dolphins and brilliantly shaded parrots yet nobody appeared to be ready to hear.

In time people got over their shock and life began to go on once more. Barges loaded with corn descended the River Weser and dumped at Hamelin. Before long storehouses were brimming with corn indeed in Hamelin. Barges brimming with wheat came up the River Weser and dumped at Hamelin. Storehouses were brimming with wheat indeed in Hamelin yet they always remembered the Pied Piper and they generally settled upon their obligations completely and on schedule.

Puss In Boots

Sometime in the distant past, there was a helpless mill operator who had three children. The years passed by and the mill operator kicked the bucket, leaving only his factory, his jackass, and a cat. The oldest child took the plant, the second-conceived child headed out on the jackass, and the most youthful child acquired the cat. "Goodness, well," said the most youthful child, "I'll eat this cat, and make a few gloves out of his hide. Then, at that point, I will have nothing left on the planet and will bite the dust of appetite."

The cat was paying attention to his king whine like this, yet he claimed not to have heard anything. However, he put on a genuine face and said: "Don't look so miserable, ace. Simply give me a pack and a couple of boots, and I will show you that you didn't get a particularly helpless legacy in me." The cat's king had regularly seen him play a large number of shrewd stunts to get rodents and mice, as when he used to hang by the heels, or conceal himself in the grain, and profess to be dead. Thoroughly considering this, he believed that it wasn't outlandish that the cat could help him, however, so he gave the cat his pack and spent his keep going pennies on requesting a fine pair of boots to be made particularly for the cat.

The cat glanced courageous in his boots, and putting his pack around his neck, he held the strings of it in his two front paws and lay by a hare warren, which was home to a considerable number of bunnies. He put wheat and corn into his pack, and extending as though he were dead, sat tight for some youthful bunnies, still not familiar with the misdirections of the world, to come and scrounge in his sack for the grain and corn.

Not long after he set down, he had what he needed. A rash and stupid youthful hare bounced into his pack, and Monsieur Puss quickly gravitated toward the strings and got him. Glad for his prey, he went with it to the royal residence and requested to talk with his highness. He was shown higher up into the ruler's condo, and making a low bow, said to him: "I have brought you, sir, a bunny of the warren, which my respectable ruler, the Marquis of Carabas (for that was the title which puss was satisfied to give his king) has directed me to present to your highness from him."

"Tell thy ace," said the king, "that I say thanks to him and that he does me a lot of joy." Another time he proceeded to shroud himself among a cornfield, keeping still his pack open, and when the support of partridges ran into it he drew the strings thus got them both. He proceeded to make a present of these to the ruler, as he had done before of the hare. The ruler, in like way, gotten the partridges with extraordinary joy and requested him some cash for a drink.

Thusly, the cat proceeded for a few months to carry presents to the ruler, continually saying that they were from his king, the Marquis of Carabas. One day specifically, he heard at the royal residence that the ruler was wanting to drive in his carriage along the stream bank, taking with him his little girl, the most excellent princess on the planet. Puss in Boots said to his king: "If you will follow my recommendation, your fortune is made. You don't have anything else to do yet proceed to wash in the stream, in the spot that I will show you, and leave the rest to me."

The mill operator's child did what the cat encouraged him to, without knowing why or wherefore. While he was washing, the ruler cruised by, and the cat started to shout out: "Help! Help! My King, Marquis of Carabas, will be suffocated!" At this commotion, the ruler put his head out of the mentoring window and discovering it was the cat who had so frequently brought him such great game, directed his watchmen to run promptly to the help of his Kingship, the Marquis of Carabas.

While they were drawing the helpless Marquis out of the stream, the cat came up to the mentor and told the ruler that while his king was washing, there dropped by certain rebels, who went off with his garments, however, he had shouted out: "Criminals! Cheats!" Multiple times, as uproarious as possible. This finesse cat had covered up the garments under an extraordinary stone. The ruler promptly told the officials of his closet to run and bring perhaps the best suit for the King Marquis of Carabas.

The ruler was exceptionally satisfied to meet the Marquis of Carabas, and the fine garments he had given him fit him amazingly well, for albeit poor, he was an attractive and a very much constructed person. The ruler's girl took a mysterious tendency to him, and the Marquis of Carabas had no sooner projected a few deferential and to some degree delicate looks however, she went gaga for him to interruption. The ruler welcomed him to sit in the mentor and ride alongside them, with the lifeguards in sparkling uniform jogging close by.

The cat, very thrilled to see his venture start to succeed, walked on previously, and meeting with some kinsmen, who were cutting a knoll, he said to them: "Great people, you who are cutting, if you don't tell the ruler that the glade you cut has a place with my King Marquis of Carabas, those warriors will slash you up like spices for the pot."

The king didn't bomb requesting from the trimmers to whom the knoll they were cutting had a place. "To my King Marquis of Carabas," addressed they through and through, for the cat's dangers had made them apprehensive. "Sir," said the Marquis, "this is a knoll which never neglects to yield a copious collect each year."

The expert cat, who went still on previously, met for certain collectors, and said to them: "Great people, you who are procuring if you don't tell the king that this corn has a place with the Marquis of Carabas, you will be cleaned up like spices for the pot." The ruler, who passed by a second after, wished to know to whom all that corn, which he then, at that point saw, had a place. "To my King Marquis of Carabas," answered the harvesters, and the ruler was all around satisfied with it, just as the Marquis, whom he saluted. Then, at that point, the ruler said: "Let us presently go to your palace."

The mill operator's child, not realizing what to answer, take a gander at puss who said: "If Your Majesty will however stand by 60 minutes, I will go on previously and request the palace to be prepared for you." With that, she bounced away and went to the palace of an extraordinary monstrosity and requested to see him, saying he was unable to pass so approach his home without having the pleasure of offering his appreciation to him. The monster got him as commonly as a monstrosity could do, and caused him to plunk down.

"I have been guaranteed," said the Cat, "that you have the endowment of having the option to change yourself into a wide range of animals as you wish; you can, for instance, change yourself into a lion, or elephant, and so forth." "That is valid," addressed the monster energetically, "and to persuade you, you will see me presently become a lion."

Puss was so frightened at seeing a lion so close to him that he quickly scaled the window ornaments, not without trouble since his boots were no utilization to him for climbing. A short time after, when Puss saw that the beast had continued his normal structure, he descended and conceded he had been particularly scared.

"In any case," said the Cat, "I dread that you won't save yourself even as a lion, for the king is accompanying his military and intends to annihilate you." The monster watched out of the window and saw the ruler holding up outside with his officers, and said: "How will I respond? How might I save myself?" Puss answered: "Assuming you can likewise change yourself into something tiny, you can cover-up."

In a moment, the monster transformed himself into a mouse and started to run about the floor. Puss no sooner saw this except for he fell upon him and gobbled him up. Puss, who heard the clamor of His Majesty's mentor running over the drawbridge, ran out and said to the ruler: "Your Majesty is welcome to this palace of my King Marquis of Carabas."

"What! My King Marquis" cried the ruler. "Does this palace likewise have a place with you? There can be nothing better than this court and every one of the masterful structures which encompass it. Release us into it, you don't mind." The Marquis gave his hand to the princess and followed the king, who went first. They passed into an extensive corridor, where they tracked down a radiant rum punch, which the beast had arranged for his companions, who were that very day to visit